THE MANCHURIAN CANDIDATE

. . . .

Greil Marcus

 Publishing

First published in 2002 by the
BRITISH FILM INSTITUTE
21 Stephen Street, London W1T 1LN

The British Film Institute
promotes greater understanding
and appreciation of, and
access to, film and moving image
culture in the UK.

British Library Cataloguing-in-Publication Data
A catalogue record for this book is available from the British Library

ISBN 0–85170–931–1

Series design by
Andrew Barron & Collis Clements Associates

Typeset in Fournier and Franklin Gothic by
D R Bungay Associates, Burghfield, Berks

Printed in Great Britain by Cromwell Press, Trowbridge, Wiltshire

CONTENTS

. . . .

For Barry Franklin

ACKNOWLEDGMENTS

. . . .

My thanks to Rob White of the British Film Institute, who invited me to take part in this series; Rachel Rosen of the San Francisco Film Festival; Wendy Lesser and *Threepenny Review*; friends Tom Luddy, Dale Block and Howard Hampton; my students in the American Studies programmes at the University of California at Berkeley and Princeton University; the Varsity Theatre in Palo Alto, California; and watchers Emily, Cecily and Jenny.

1

A LITTLE SOLITAIRE

A popular Chinese magazine proposed, in a plot not unlike 'The Manchurian Candidate,' that Lewinsky had been sent to Washington when she was a child as a Cold War agent on a mission to entrap the president and destabilize the government. 'Is Lewinsky with the KGB?' inquired the headline ... Meantime, the Syrian defense minister, too, announced that the affair was a Zionist plot. 'Monica Lewinsky is a young Jewish girl that Mossad hired and pushed into working as an intern in the White House.'

> Marjorie Garber, 'Moniker', in *Our Monica, Ourselves: The Clinton Affair and the National Interest*, edited by Lauren Berlant and Lisa Duggan (New York University Press, 2001)

When Nixon needed to think, he picked up a legal pad and wrote outlines. Reagan composed letters. Clinton played solitaire.

> George Stephanopoulos, review of *Reaching for Glory: Lyndon Johnson's Secret White House Tapes, 1964–1965*, *New York Times Book Review*, 30 December 2001

A voice: 'Raymond, why don't you pass the time by playing a little solitaire?' The question is a command, and the first trigger. The thin, dark-haired man takes up a pack of card and begins to lay them out. He turns up the Queen of Diamonds. It is the second trigger. Once it shows, as the dark-haired man will say when it is too late, 'They can make me do anything, can't they?'

Eleanor Iselin (Angela Lansbury) and Raymond Shaw (Laurence Harvey), near the end (left); Major Ben Marco (Frank Sinatra), the end (right).

13

2

. . . .

IN 2001

Yet suppose instead of *G.I. Blues* he had been cast in *The Manchurian Candidate*, a film that captures the secret, encrypted side of Presleyan myth: the shellshocked, brainwashed soldier as a version of the post-Army Elvis, even as the widespread belief that rock 'n' roll was a communist plot fits snugly into the movie's conspiratorial milieu. And surely Angela Lansbury suggests a deliciously malign composite of Presley's ruthless manager Col. Tom Parker and his adored mother Gladys – a living military-industrial Oedipus complex.

Howard Hampton, 'Scorpio Descending', *Film Comment*, March–April 1997

I tried to use Pavlov to get him to stop the war. Conditioning, behaviorism ... 'The Manchurian Candidate,' have you seen it? ... I tried to get him to forge an association, 'peace,' 'Quaker,' 'Mom.' Now I see it was just the wrong series of associations. That *mother*.

Tony Kushner, obituary for Dr Arnold Hutschnecker, 'A Shrink in Paradise: Nixon's confidant takes to the couch inside the Pearly Gates', *New York Times Magazine*, 30 December 2001

When a movie has become part of the folklore of a nation, the borders between the movie and the nation cease to exist. The movie becomes a fable; then it becomes a metaphor. Then it becomes a catchphrase, a joke, a shortcut. It becomes a way not to think, and all the details of the movie, everything that made it stick in people's minds, that brought it to life not just on the screen but in the imagination of the people at large, no matter how few or many those details might be, dissolve. The catchphrase contains the movie, and both become meaningless. Speak the words: they have become a way of saying, *We've seen it all before*. Unless you haven't seen the movie.

When *The Manchurian Candidate* was presented at the San Francisco Film Festival in 2001, as part of a programme of films from earlier festivals – in this case, from 1962 – the crowd was mostly under forty. The picture was about a plot to assassinate a presidential candidate; taken out of circulation after the assassination of President John F. Kennedy in 1963, it was rereleased both theatrically and on video in 1988 to great acclaim. Now it was about to unspool in the Castro Theatre, an ornately baroque movie palace with a steep balcony and an organ that emerges from a pit in front of the stage.

The theatre creates an atmosphere of anticipation; it sparks the feeling that, whatever might be on the bill, something extraordinary is about to take place. 'This picture invites you in for a cool night of suspense and leaves you with no ground beneath your feet,' the audience had been told, but as the film began, the titters and open laughter made two things clear: first, that it's easy to forget that *The Manchurian Candidate* is, among other things, a comedy, and, second, that the people laughing had no idea what was coming.

3
. . . .
IN 1959

1961 Sinatra getting peeved at Kennedy Brothers. Being pushed aside because of Mafia connections. 9/24/61 Sinatra at Hyanis Port, then to Tell Robert and John to get off Sam Giancana case in Chicago … AT THAT POINT, SINATRA TOLD PRESIDENT KENNEDY ABOUT HIS INTEREST IN MAKING THE MOVIE 'MANCHURIAN CANDIDATE' … This movie not too veiled threat to JFK after rejection by Bobby, Justice Dept …

> Mae Brussell, World Watchers International Tape #860,
> 30 May 1998

The network of businessmen, agents and gangsters that links Bill Clinton to China's Communist dictatorship is interwoven with every element of the greatest security disaster in American history. It as though the Rosenbergs were in the White House, except that the Rosenbergs were little people and naïve, and consequently the damage they were capable of accomplishing was incomparably less.

> David Horowitz, 'The Manchurian Candidate', *Salon*,
> 21 June 1999

Published in 1959, Richard Condon's novel *The Manchurian Candidate* had an unusual kind of success. It was simultaneously a bestseller and a cult book, casual reading for the public and the subject of hushed conversations among sophisticates: could this really happen?

The timing seemed safe. Dwight D. Eisenhower was nearing the end of his second term as president: 'Things,' as he once put it, were 'more like they are now than they ever were before.' Senator Joseph McCarthy had been dead since 1957. Five years had passed since the Senate that once followed his lead had cut him down with an overwhelming vote of censure. It was easy to forget the great days of 1950, when the then-obscure Republican from Wisconsin stood before a crowd in Wheeling, West Virginia, to charge that there were 205 traitorous members of the Communist Party in the State Department, and that the State Department knew it; when he rose on the floor of the Senate itself not two weeks later to speak for six hours in defence of his nation, then putting himself forward as the leader the nation deserved but did not have, challenging every agency of government and every citizen to stand in his light; when he bestrode like a colossus a land where, finally, all were equal – where no one was above suspicion. But in 1954 McCarthy had gone too far. He accused the Army itself of espionage, refused to reveal his evidence, and in an instant the cry 'Have you no shame?' turned into 'The Emperor has no clothes.' McCarthy had helped turn the United States into a haunted house where you could watch as your fellow citizens were named as turncoats, fellow-travellers, subversives, degenerates – where, even more thrillingly, you yourself might be seized from the gaping crowd – but now the show was over.

The nation turned away from the false charges, from the threatened, bribed or merely lying witnesses, from the whole industry of exposure, and everyone awoke from what all were happy to assure each other had been like a dream. But *what if?* Condon was now so playfully asking in his book – what if Joe McCarthy was really working for the Russians and the Chinese, for the very Communists he was supposedly attempting to destroy? And what if behind such a man lay a genius even more evil than he – say, the senator's own wife, pulling his strings? And what if, in the conspiracy they served, there was the wife's own son, like other American GIs taken prisoner during the Korean War somehow made to turn against his own country, but here far more profoundly, psychologically remade as an assassin-in-waiting, with no knowledge of the role he is to play? And what if his role is to kill in just such a manner as to propel Condon's putatively anti-Communist demagogue into the White House, so that he might turn the country over to its enemies? And then the big question: could anyone stop a conspiracy so brilliant, so perfect, so absurd, that no one would believe it?

That was Richard Condon's game in *The Manchurian Candidate*, and the novel was so purposefully crass, so self-consciously superior both to its tale and its audience, that you didn't have to believe it. There was one moment when the book seemed to go through its own looking glass – when, as you read, you could imagine the country looking at itself. 'This country is going to go through a fire like it has never seen,' the senator's wife says to her son in words that will be wiped from his mind as completely as any sense of what he has become. 'Time,' she says, 'is going to roar and flash lightning in the streets, Raymond. Blood will gush behind the noise and stones will fall and fools and mockers will be brought down. The smugness and complacency of this country will be dragged through the blood and noise in the streets until it becomes a country purged and purified.' But that was an odd break in the underlying contempt of the book for its own actors, in the fog a writer leaves behind when he is bored with his own story – where, in Condon's pages, he cannot even summon enough respect for his characters to allow them the stage they supposedly occupy, when the nation the writer's Joe McCarthy is supposed to command turns into 'a group for anthropologists', gathering from 'ten thousand yesterdays in the Middle West and neolithic Texas'. They didn't scare the reader, and neither did the book. That the story would lodge in the nation's pysche and stay there was the work of other hands.

4

....

IN 1954

If you come in five minutes after this picture begins, you won't know
what it's all about!

Poster for *The Manchurian Candidate*, 1962

It's 1954. Major Ben Marco of the US Army, played by Frank Sinatra, is
lying on his bed, fully clothed in his uniform, dreaming the same dream
he dreams every night. He's sweating. As his lips twitch, the camera
moves in and we enter his dream.

We're in an old hotel in Spring Lake, New Jersey; a meeting of the
Ladies Garden Club is in progress. On a small stage, one Mrs Henry
Whittaker, on her feet, is speaking from behind a small white table; seated
on either side of her are all the members of the patrol that Major Marco,
then Captain Marco, led in Korea in 1952. The soldiers look bored out of
their minds. The talk they're listening to, that we're listening to, is
beyond boring: 'Fun with Hydrangeas.' The scene is striking – the
ghastliness of Mrs Whittaker's floral print dress is topped only by her
hat – and you only subliminally register what's off about it. Something in
the way Mrs Whittaker is speaking is too harsh. She's disdainful,
mocking, as if the other Ladies Garden Club members, whom we haven't
yet seen but whom Mrs Whittaker is presumably addressing, are fools.

The camera begins a circular pan around the room: now we see Mrs
Whittaker's audience, women dressed just like her, most of them over
fifty, a few young, listening attentively, taking notes, whispering politely
to each other. It's a long, slow pan, and when the camera returns to Mrs
Whittaker the scene is completely different.

Yen Lo, a fat, entertaining scientist from the Pavlov Institute in
Moscow, played by Khigh Dhiegh, is now speaking. As in the New
Jersey Hotel, the soldiers from Major Marco's platoon are seated on
either side of the speaker, but now in a small, steep, modern
auditorium; the seats are filled with Soviet and Chinese cadres. Behind
Yen Lo are huge photos of Mao, Stalin, workers, peasants – an
ultramodern, post-Constructivist montage of great style and elegance.
You notice Yen Lo's drooping moustache and his terrible teeth; light
gleams off his shaved skull.

Yen Lo explains that the soldiers – betrayed by their interpreter, Chunjin, played by Henry Silva – were set up for an ambush while on manoeuvres in Korea, then flown by helicopter to a centre in Manchuria where Yen Lo has, as he puts it, condescendingly citing endless scholarly monographs from the previous half-century, 'conditioned them – or *brainwashed* them', he says, laughing, 'which I understand is the new American word'. The soldiers, Yen Lo says to his audience, as if telling an inside joke, which for that matter he is, have been made to believe that they are waiting out a storm in a New Jersey hotel. Whatever Yen Lo says, all they hear is flower talk.

Mrs Whittaker reappears – speaking Yen Lo's words in her own voice, but even more harshly than before, with an edge of contempt. Behind her are portraits of Stalin and Mao.

Yen Lo appears as himself in the auditorium. He speaks as himself, in the New Jersey hotel. From his point of view, we see the audience, the Ladies Garden Club. Mrs Whittaker speaks Yen Lo's words in the auditorium. In the hotel, Yen Lo speaks as Yen Lo, with Communist cadres filling the garden club seats.

In the audience, a cadaverous Russian demands an end to Yen Lo's pedantic accounts of the invention of false memories, the creation of secondary personalities, the Pavlov Institute's successes in deterministic manipulative response, the naïve American belief that men and women cannot be conditioned to act against their true selves – Yen Lo, or Mrs Whittaker, has lost himself, or herself, in footnotes and bibliographies. The question, the man in the audience says, is Sergeant Raymond Shaw, a stiff, effetely accented prig played by Laurence Harvey – who, in the opening minutes of *The Manchurian Candidate*, we've seen returning to the United States from Korea to be awarded the Congressional Medal of Honor, for leading his supposedly lost patrol back to safety. The question is, says the Russian in the audience, 'Has the man ever killed anyone?'

Mrs Whittaker asks Raymond Shaw – seated just forward from his fellow soldiers, not slumped in his chair as they are, but with his back straight and assiduously making repeated, deliberate hand motions on the speaker's table – if he has ever killed anyone. 'No, Ma'am,' he says quietly, as if wondering why anyone would ask such a question. 'Not even in combat?' says Yen Lo as himself, in the garden club. 'In combat? Yes, Ma'am, I think so,' Shaw says, as if in awe at the notion, or to banish the thought. A smiling member of the garden club is cradling a bayonet

Marco's dream, Marco's
memory

like a kitten. Mrs Whittaker, speaking as Yen Lo, is about to take it, when a Russian officer, in the auditorium, objects: 'Not with the knife, with the hands.' The officer turns into a member of the garden club, gaily waving a handkerchief.

Yen Lo is present in the auditorium as himself. To prove the efficacy of the work he has done on Shaw and the others, Raymond, who, Yen Lo has explained, has been programmed as an assassin who will have no memory of his deeds, will now have to kill the member of the patrol he least dislikes – in one of the first scenes of the film we have seen him rousting his patrol from a whorehouse, hatred for him on their faces, disgust for them on his. 'Captain Marco,' Shaw says. 'No,' says Mrs Whittaker, with Stalin and Mao looming behind her. 'We need him to get you your medal.' So Shaw chooses the soldier he least dislikes after Marco, and begins to strangle him with a towel the Russian officer has brought to the stage. The soldier protests: 'No, no, Ed,' Yen Lo says in a friendly voice. The soldier ceases to resist; it's just one more moment in 'Fun with Hydrangeas'. Throughout the sequence, the soldiers have acted naturally, not at all like zombies, just bored. So now this soldier is, again, bored.

Raymond Shaw kills him, and the dead man topples off his chair. No one reacts. It is 1952; back in 1954, Major Marco wakes up screaming.

The Twilight Zone

What we've seen is unlike any other dream sequence in film history: nothing before it bears comparison, and nothing afterward.

Think of the work Salvador Dalí and Alfred Hitchcock did in *Spellbound*, playing out formal Surrealist dream-notions, notions that by 1945 were already a visual cliché: in a dream, one thing melts into another. Compared to the bizarre series of shots in *The Manchurian Candidate*, where images seem to accumulate until like a house of cards they tumble and, at least in the viewer's mind, the search for epistemological coherence and stability has to begin all over again, the result of the Dalí–Hitchcock collaboration is visually florid and intellectually dead. It's as dead as it was in the principal on-screen dream-work that, in the United States, directly preceded *The Manchurian Candidate*: beginning in 1959, the first four seasons of Rod Serling's television show *The Twilight Zone*. Working budgets so low that even 1950s viewers often laughed over the obvious attempts of the writers to stick to a single set, dreams were merely realistic: it only took a dissolve to take you into a parallel reality, where everything was just as it was before, except that, say, no one knew your name. In both *Spellbound*, with what was at least paraded as the most sophisticated account of dreams in cinema, and *The Twilight Zone*, which could not even afford to humour the psychoanalytic vogue of the 1950s, relying more on the lingering traces of magic and witchery in the mind of the time, the people behind the camera pretend they know what a dream is, how it works, what it is for: keys to hidden individual or social fears and desires, or anyway clues to the mysteries of the plot. But in *The Manchurian Candidate*, even to describe Major Marco's dream as a dream is to cheat, to dodge the question, to use a shortcut that, finally, only takes you back where you began.

The sequence is set up as a dream, but it doesn't come off the screen as a dream, as a blur, with soft edges or milky tones in its images. There are no lacunae, self-cancelling actions or logical gaps in its narrative. Is it a dream, emerging out of Marco's existence as a subjective individual, out of his own fears and desires – or is it altogether objective, a displaced but absolutely accurate memory of a constructed situation in which, like an actor fed lines through a chip implanted in his brain, Marco once played a part? Is it a subjective shuffling of marked cards that were objectively dealt to produce a specific hand – a shuffling that now, against the dealer's original intent, has produced a hand that is not quite what it was supposed to be? Why is the sequence so cold, so funny, so horrible, so pleased with its refusal, even at its moment of death, to resolve its fundamental contradiction, between one narrator who, emotionally, must be real, and another who, in real-life terms, cannot be – and vice versa? Why is it so austere?

A Lunatic Force

The sequence is structured around the same modernist principles that, boiled down to propaganda images still more imbued with the delirium of the avant-garde than the functionalism of socialist realism, shape the photo-montage backdrop Yen Lo and Mrs Whittaker speak against. These are the principles, the art historian T. J. Clark wrote in 1999 in *Farewell to an Idea*, by which modern artists responded to – and sought to defeat – modernity. In France, Italy, Russia, Germany, Switzerland and the United States, certain artists told a story about the failure of ordinary languages and images to account for a world that – after the French Revolution and the mostly successful attempt of the nineteenth century to proceed as if no revolution had ever taken place, after the Battle of the Somme and the Great Crash of 1929 – no longer even pretended to make sense. The modern economy and modern warfare, rushing forward like a flood, and with no more eyes than a flood, erased all certainty, all ritual, all the old music of everyday life. Against that overwhelming noise of modernity, modernists countered with a drive towards silence and abstraction, and with a nihilist manifesto: nothing can be said, nothing can be seen, not for more than an instant; nothing will hold still. As a response to the blindness of modernity, modernists tried to make the world see through modern eyes: sightless eyes.

'Blindness, purposelessness, randomness, blankness,' Clark wrote, catching Kasimir Malevich's 1915 Suprematist black squares; the secret alphabets and unknown tongues of El Lissitzky's 1919 Prouns; or catching Hans Arp, who in 1916 found himself in Zurich, ripping up his work, throwing the pieces into the air, and deciding the picture of the world that he would affirm was true was the pattern the pieces made when they hit the ground. 'It is not for us to see how the new world will be built,' El Lissitzky announced when the Soviet Union was new, when he still believed artists were as likely to shape its future as dictators and bureaucrats. 'It will not be built with our knowledge and technology. It will be built with a direct and accurate force – a lunatic force, from which all will recoil in shame' – and as modern people, we understand such ideas even when we claim that we don't. We run from the world those ideas imply because we know what it is – and when presented with a version as complete and as implacable as the montage of shots in *The Manchurian Candidate*, one is sucked all the way in.

The sequence is visually irresistible – lucid, as anything beautiful is lucid. At the same time it's unacceptable – confusing, at first, then an impossibility, then perfectly possible. As dramatised by the gestures and speech of the people within it, the action is completely naturalistic. As a game, the sequence plays according to rules as self-reinforcing as they are strict. The tableau is most of all severe. As a story it is mathematical: a fact, true. You realise that in the world posited by the movie, this actually happened.

A Sense of Dread

It's here, in this moment, that *The Manchurian Candidate*, a black-and-white Hollywood movie directed by John Frankenheimer, written by George Axelrod, takes off. It's here that you realise something is happening on the screen that you haven't seen before, that you're not ready for. Even if you've read the book, you aren't ready. All Condon made up of the movie's beginning was the setting – the soldiers in the hotel – a setting which in the book lies flat, like Condon's dialogue, so much of it used word-for-word in the film, alive and frightening on the screen, dead in print. Condon imagined none of the cinematic shifts that nail the details of the event into your mind, the shifts that scramble the event, that make its details almost impossible to keep straight. You sense, suddenly, that this movie you're watching, a movie that promised no more than an evening's good time, can go anywhere, in any direction – you sense that there's no way to predict what's going to happen next, how it's going to happen, why it's going to happen.

In the theatre in San Francisco in 2001, the ghosts of the past had begun to gather over the crowd. As the film moved into its progressive, real-time plot, following Sinatra's Major Marco and Harvey's Raymond Shaw into the United States in a presidential election year, people in the audience seemed to forget the displacement of Marco's dream, again laughing easily over Raymond's undisguised loathing for Eleanor Iselin, his ridiculously overbearing mother, played by Angela Lansbury, and his boorish, alcoholic stepfather, the Red-baiting US Senator John Iselin, played by James Gregory, or the way Rosie, a tough-looking woman played by Janet Leigh, picks up Marco outside the club car of a train after his torturing dream or his accursed memories have led to his mental and physical collapse and his departure from the Army, the only life he has ever known.

With a bizarre lack of surprise, an almost clinical curiosity, she watches as Marco, twitching in his civilian clothes as if he'd found them in a costume store, goes to pieces before her eyes. He puts a cigarette to his lips and it drops out of his mouth and into his drink, takes another cigarette but can't lift his shaking hand to his mouth, then rises in shame, knocks his drink to the floor, and rushes out of the car as if to throw up in the lavatory, or jump from the moving train. Joining Marco in the vestibule, Rosie unreels a string of bad puns and non sequiturs so weird you begin to wonder if she is not in fact an agent sent to run a now-defenceless Marco himself – she seems to be conducting a random search for the spoken trigger that will allow her to replace Yen Lo's version of Marco's mind with her own – until she frankly offers herself to him in a manner that, filtered through the mores of 1962, or even 2001, is as absurd as the action taking place in the New Jersey hotel, and just as believable. But while this scene and so many others around it were comic, tapping into the Freudian shtick of 1950s black humour – as with a plainly disintegrating Marco explaining to his commanding officer, that yes, he really has read every one of the hundreds of books littering his apartment, from *Modern French Theatre* to *Ethnic Choices of the Arabs* to *Diseases of Horses* to *Jurisprudential Factor of Mafia Administration* – a sense of dread had now been loaded into every movement of a character from one room to another, into every line of dialogue.

As Sinatra and Marco, Dhiegh and Yen Lo, Harvey and Shaw, Lansbury and Mrs Iselin, Gregory and Senator Iselin, and Leigh and Rosie stepped into their story, it was as if each of them had a shade, or a whole coven of them: John F. Kennedy and Lee Harvey Oswald, Oswald and Jack Ruby, Malcolm X and Elijah Muhammad, Martin Luther King, Jr. and James Earl Ray, Robert F. Kennedy and Sirhan Sirhan, Andy Warhol and Valerie Solanas, George Wallace and Arthur Bremer,

John F. Kennedy

Lee Harvey Oswald

Jack Ruby

Malcolm X

Elijah Muhammad

Martin Luther King, Jr

James Earl Ray

Robert F. Kennedy

Sirhan Sirhan

Andy Warhol

Valerie Solanas

George Wallace

Arthur Bremer

Leo Ryan

Jim Jones

George Moscone

Harvey Milk

Dan White

John Lennon

Mark Chapman

Ronald Reagan

John Hinkley

Gerald Ford

Squeaky Fromme

Sarah Jane Moore

Alan Berg (courtesy *The Denver Post*)

David Lane of the Order

Congressman Leo Ryan and Jim Jones, George Moscone and Harvey Milk and Dan White, John Lennon and Mark Chapman, Ronald Reagan and John Hinckley. There were countless more, depending on who your mind turned up: Sarah Jane Moore and Squeaky Fromme, would-be assassins of Gerald Ford, or Alan Berg, the Denver talk-show host murdered by the fascist brotherhood the Order, if in fact your mind could hold onto the facts, hold onto the names, if in truth they didn't begin to move like Mrs Whittaker and Yen Lo, Jim Jones appearing as a trusted advisor to JFK, John Lennon spending a night of his 'Lost Weekend' with Squeaky Fromme, Sirhan Sirhan running drugs for Jack Ruby, Arthur Bremer passing out campaign literature for Ronald Reagan, and on, and on, and on, out of the shadows of the years that had followed the movie, and back into the film. Yes, the 'Manchurian Candidate' had long since become a joke in itself, but now, in the theatre, every laugh had an echo.

You couldn't tell the echoes from the jokes; maybe that was why people kept laughing, as Raymond Shaw said 'Make like a housewife!' to Jocelyn Jordan, his new wife, played by a forgotten Leslie Parrish; as his stepfather, dressed as Abraham Lincoln, and his mother, dressed as a milkmaid, presided over a costume party that Raymond Shaw's soon-to-be father-in-law, the liberal US Senator Thomas Jordan, played by John McGiver, calls a 'fascist rally'; as Yen Lo discussed the finances of the KGB's front business in New York; even after the jittery impatience of Eleanor Iselin's every word or movement had lost its comic silliness and Angela Lansbury's teeth had plainly changed into fangs.

5

. . . .

IN 1962

Fenton Bresler suggests in his book *Who Killed John Lennon* that
Mark Chapman had been brainwashed to serve as a 'Manchurian
Candidate' to kill the prolific counter-culture leader.

> Klint Finley, 'Imagine This: John Lennon Assassination
> Theories', technoccult.net, 2000

The Columbine killings were the beginning of the final push to take
all guns out of the hands of the American people … The only way to
stop these shootings is to make the public realize that 'Manchurian
Candidates' do exist, and the kids who are committing these tragic
crimes are victims of government mind control. The purpose of the
shootings is to inflame the public against guns so that they force
Congress to pass restrictive gun laws. Once the guns are out of the
hands of the American public, another twist in random mayhem will
begin. More programmed 'Manchurian Candidates' will begin
anarchistic attacks on the public using bombs, knives, fires, Molotov
cocktails, baseball bats and any other item that can be used as a
weapon. Anarchy will sweep the streets of the United States …
If this happens in 1999 or the year 2000, Bill and Hillary Clinton will
be the permanent totalitarian rulers of the United States!

> 'Mind Control in Amerika: Five Easy Steps to Create a
> Manchurian Candidate', rumormillnews.com, 2000

The Manchurian Candidate stands as the most exciting American movie
from *Citizen Kane* to the first two *Godfather* pictures because the opening
dream sequence is not a set-piece, not a matter of a director showing off
his cleverness, a cinematographer flaunting deep focus or a set designer
parading his flair for matching décor – though all of those things are
surely present. That sequence is a promise the movie pays in full. To see
Raymond Shaw strangle the soldier – and later, in another patrol
member's matching dream, to see Shaw shoot a second soldier, to see the
wash of his blood and brain matter splatter Stalin's face – is to be
shocked, and not to be prepared for the atrocities that follow: much
quieter, almost silent atrocities, and all the worse for that. And yet the

shock is, in a sense, immaculate: 'I have written a wicked book,' Herman Melville wrote to Nathaniel Hawthorne about *Moby-Dick*, 'and feel spotless as the lamb.' That's the feeling: a simultaneous imprisonment and liberation, all outside of history, or anyway the moment in which the film was made – as that moment understood itself.

While the person watching has been made a prisoner of the movie's drama, he or she has not been made a subject of manipulation, not positioned to accept this argument for that reason, even to take sides for or against one character or another. Whatever the pacing of a given segment of the film, something inside of the film is moving too fast for that. That something, you sense, might be a history that the intelligence inside the movie has felt, but not understood, not even tried to understand, repeating to itself, *Don't analyse, dramatise!* Trapped in the film, you can feel most stranded by the realisation that there is no message here, no point being made, not even any particular implication that foreign Communists are bad and Americans are good, nothing like that whatsoever – this is all, somehow, taking place in an atmosphere of geopolitical neutrality, of aesthetic suspension. (United Artists was afraid of the film because it was concerned that if a détente between the United States and the Soviet Union were to be emerging at the time of the picture's release, the movie might embarrass President Kennedy. 'They said [it was] anti-Russian,' George Axelrod recalled in 1988, 'which it wasn't.' 'Of course not,' Frankenheimer said.) The picture floats free of the busy cycle of American Cold War films, be they gross propaganda or auteurist touchstones. It's too daring, too stylish, in the context of its time too nihilist to play in the Cold War Film Festival alongside the likes of *Shack Out on 101*, *My Son John*, *I Married a Communist*, *Pickup on South Street*, *The Iron Curtain*, *Night People*, *Invasion U.S.A.*, *I Was a Communist for the F.B.I.* – or even *From Russia with Love*.

We're not seeing a film that wants us to agree with it. We're seeing John Frankenheimer, George Axelrod, the cinematographer Lionel Lindon, the production designer Richard Sylbert, the composer David Amram, and Sinatra, Harvey, Lansbury, Leigh, Dhiegh, McGiver, Gregory, and a clutch of actors in smaller roles – the actor playing the sallow head of the KGB's New York section, or the Army psychiatrist, or Marco's commanding officer, or Mrs Whittaker – working over their heads, diving into material they've chosen, or been given, and in every case outstripping the material and themselves.

The Highest Note

Before and after *The Manchurian Candidate* John Frankenheimer was an efficient director whose movies mostly vanished when you walked out of the theatre; his most distinctive work has come in thrillers of various degrees of cheesiness. Born in New York in 1930, he worked in film while in the Air Force and in 1954 began directing live TV. In 1957, for the prestigious *Playhouse 90* showcase, he made 'The Comedian', one of many Rod Serling scripts he directed, starring Mickey Rooney as a cruel, domineering star who cannot love. 'Someone once asked me, "How were you able to do such quality stuff then, compared what what television does now?"' Frankenheimer said in 1995 to the critic Charles Champlin. 'The answer is that most people didn't own a television set in those days. Owning a TV set was a kind of elitist thing, and we had an elitist audience.' But as a movie director he did not work for an elitist audience, and if twenty-eight years after *The Manchurian Candidate* he was making *The Holcroft Covenant*, an incestuous-Nazis-plot-to-rule-the-world picture in which hero Michael Caine looks embarrassed in almost every shot, it was different mostly in kind from what had preceded it, or what would follow.

There was *Seven Days in May* in 1964, a liberal cautionary tale about a military coup in the United States, with a script by Serling; in 1966, *Seconds*, a *Twilight Zone* episode blown up to big-picture scale and starring a confused-looking Rock Hudson; the 1977 *Black Sunday*, an

John Frankenheimer (left) and George Axelrod

expert, glamorous tracking of a terrorist plan to attack the Super Bowl, with Bruce Dern in the most convincing of his many deranged Vietnam veteran roles; cable TV movies about the 1971 Attica prison revolt, the murder of Brazilian rainforest activist Chico Mendes and the attempted assassination of George Wallace. In 2000, at seventy, Frankenheimer made the decadent, creepily empty *Reindeer Games*, a heavily promoted Ben Affleck vehicle notable mainly as one of a whole series of films in which Charlize Theron ends up dead, probably because she has more screen presence than her male leads can tolerate. In 2002 he made *Path to War*, an HBO film about Lyndon Johnson and Vietnam starring Michael Gambon as Johnson as King Lear.

In *The Manchurian Candidate* there are scores of shots, scenes, framed gestures – or lines that by their blunt isolation on the screen as they are spoken carry over from one sequence to the next like the way Wayne Perkins's guitar solo in the Wailers' 'Concrete Jungle' reaches its highest note only after Bob Marley takes back the song – that have more affective, mnemonic power than in the rest of Frankenheimer's work piled on top of itself: as in the very first shot of *The Manchurian Candidate*, when in pitch darkness Laurence Harvey's Sergeant Shaw drives an empty transport vehicle up to the Korean brothel, gets out and strides towards the door while Sinatra's Captain Marco waits in the passenger seat, watching as Shaw passes by, looking at him as if he's never seen anything stranger, more out of place, in his life. It's just something in the eyes.

Four Actors

Laurence Harvey, born in Janiskis, Lithuania, in 1928, dead of cancer in 1973, made a career out of playing neurasthenics; Jeremy Irons in the last scene of *Damage*, an exile with no company but his own narcissistic self-loathing, could be summing up almost the whole of Harvey's career, from his most effective (*A Dandy in Aspic*, 1968) to his most miserablist (*Room at the Top*, 1959). 'What more can you say of a man most interesting as a zombie?' David Thomson wrote in *A Biographical Dictionary of Film*. You can say that in *The Manchurian Candidate* Harvey, like Al Pacino as Michael Corleone in *The Godfather Part II*, kept his character in such an Iron Maiden of repression that there may be nothing in the film so frightening as the moment when, with his very last words in the picture, he speaks as a human being, as a man possessed – as a man possessed, finally, by himself. Despite the wonderful scene where

Marco gets Raymond Shaw drunk and Harvey slides his character into a sodden reverie, or his proud insistence that no matter how much the men in his platoon hated him it was nothing compared to the hatred he had for them, it is only in this last moment, when the story has come to an end, that the chill leaves the character Harvey has made: that he has played from the inside out.

For all of that, Harvey's performance may not be as strange as Janet Leigh's, from the inside out not of her character but of the movie itself, if not simply floating above the surface of the film, never quite connecting at all – you can't tell. Born in 1927 in Merced, California, in the Central Valley, she became a screen immortal because of the 1959 *Psycho*, but for Hitchcock's editing of her butchering, not her acting – not for anything like the now banal, now cryptic, ultimately unreadable person Leigh becomes in *The Manchurian Candidate*. There are reserves of experience in her face, in the way she moves or, especially, doesn't. When in the vestibule of the train her Rosie tells Sinatra's Marco, 'I was one of the original Chinese workmen who laid the track on this straight,' Leigh is so solid on her feet the absurdity doesn't necessarily register.

Rosie (Janet Leigh) and Ben Marco in the club car

In the vestibule

You almost wonder why she doesn't look Chinese – or, the second or third time through the picture, if the word 'Chinese' is a clue. 'Maryland is a beautiful state,' she says. 'This is Delaware,' Sinatra says blankly. 'Maryland is a beautiful state,' she says again, as if 'Maryland' is the key to his lock. 'So is Ohio, for that matter,' she says; maybe *that's* it. This Janet Leigh reappears nowhere in her own career, but only in the person of Deborah Harry's Nicki Brand in David Cronenberg's 1983 *Videodrome* – and even there, in a film closely modelled on *The*

Manchurian Candidate, compared to Leigh's Rosie, Harry's cool sado-masochist, playing James Woods's brainwashed assassin like a piano, is as easy to read as a stop sign.

With nearly forty movie roles between 1941 and 1961, Frank Sinatra, born in Hoboken, New Jersey, in 1915, dead in 1998, was sometimes a good actor, sometimes more than that, instinctive and wary, but his film career mostly suggested he had nothing better to do with himself – even though, with the Capitol recordings that peaked in 1959 with *No One Cares*, he obviously did. In that album, especially on his bottomless version of Bunny Berigan's 1937 'I Can't Get Started', he tapped into a well of melancholy, summoning a sense of despair he was never able to carry into film – or was never moved to do so – until the last shot and the last words of *The Manchurian Candidate*. Despite his Private Maggio in *From Here to Eternity* in 1953 (a one-note performance; nemesis Ernest Borgnine is better), Frankie Machine in *The Man with the Golden Arm* from 1954 (an impossibly stagey, set-bound film, with every movement telegraphed by another, and Sinatra's struggling junkie not that much more interesting than his Snidely Whiplash dealer; only Kim Novak seems real), or the 1957 *Pal Joey* (where Sinatra's Nathan Detroit from the 1955 *Guys and Dolls* turned into a convincingly irresistible heel), Sinatra's movies often played like publicity for his music, or as a reach for a validation that war, politics or crime can provide, but art cannot: the certainty that one matters, or that the lives of others depend on yours. Without its meaningless thematic link to *The Manchurian Candidate*, there would be no reason to remember *Suddenly*, the 1954 picture in which Sinatra plays a would-be presidential assassin – a plodding movie, supposedly seen by Lee Harvey Oswald only days before John F. Kennedy was shot, where, without motive or characterisation, not a lot more seems to be at stake than with the elaborately pointless assassination attempt on the undescribed diplomat in either of Hitchcock's versions of *The Man Who Knew Too Much*.

Sinatra made eighteen pictures after *The Manchurian Candidate*; not one can support the weight of his panic when he realises the story Raymond Shaw is carrying is crashing towards its end and he cannot stop it. Sinatra had to know his life in the movies would rest with this one film. He had ownership of the rights to reissue the picture seven years after its initial release, rights that, in 1962, were worthless ('A picture played on television and it was over,' as Frankenheimer put it to Charles Champlin in 1995). In 1988, when United Artists wanted to put the film out on video, Sinatra insisted it be rereleased theatrically; when the studio refused, he put up two million dollars of his own money as a guarantee.

It was George Axelrod who suggested to Frankenheimer that they look at Richard Condon's novel. They read it together and, the property having been turned down all over Hollywood as too explosive, secured the rights that same day, each putting up $5,000 against a purchase price of $75,000. Again at their own expense, they flew to Florida to approach Sinatra, offering him his choice of roles. With Sinatra on board, they were close to a studio commitment, but it apparently took Sinatra's intercession with President Kennedy and a call from Kennedy to Arthur Krim, head of both the Democratic National Committee and of United Artists, which controlled distribution of Sinatra pictures, to overcome United Artists' resistance to the project. Kennedy had read the book himself. 'Who plays the mother?' he supposedly asked Sinatra; Sinatra wanted Lucille Ball. It's impossible not to try to think the notion through, to imagine Ball matching Martha Raye in Chaplin's *Monsieur Verdoux* – to imagine Ball, with her *I Love Lucy* years already over, not only leaving behind a beloved American icon, but a witch looking out from her batting eyes.

Frankenheimer wanted Angela Lansbury, with whom he'd worked in his serious family drama *All Fall Down*, finished in 1962 just before work on *The Manchurian Candidate* was to begin. The film convinced Sinatra – but in *All Fall Down* Lansbury's controlling mother is merely hysterical in her desperate attempt to make sure that no one ever does anything wrong; it's *her* problem. The performance is only steps away from her Eleanor Iselin, who is our problem, but they are steps from one world into another. Born in London in 1925, Lansbury was only three years older than Laurence Harvey; as the mother in *All Fall Down*, she seems older than the mother in *The Manchurian Candidate*. At the same time, the mother of *All Fall Down*'s callow Warren Beatty could never have been the mother of the frozen, terrified Laurence Harvey. Lansbury had to be both older and younger – more powerful, more sexual, more intelligent, more loving, more cruel. How did she do it? How do you not doubt for an instant that Lansbury's Eleanor Iselin gave birth to Harvey's Raymond, and that the camera must cut away from the kiss she gives him as she sends him off to perdition for the same reason a camera in 1962 always had to cut away from a kiss? She might have turned herself into Agatha Christie's Miss Marple for *The Mirror Crack'd* in

1980 and Jessica Fletcher for the 1984–91 television series *Murder, She Wrote* simply to erase the memory of Eleanor Iselin's crimes – God knows, Marple and Fletcher couldn't have solved them. Lansbury never came close to what she did in *The Manchurian Candidate* before, and she never came close again.

A Special Thrill

You could say the same for almost anyone involved in the project. Something – something in the story, something in the times, in the interplay of various people caught up consciously in the story, and consciously, unconsciously or half-consciously in the times – came together, with the challenges and warnings of John F. Kennedy's inaugural address still lodged in the hearts of those making the movie: 'In the long history of the world, only a few generations have been granted the role of defending freedom in its hour of maximum danger. I do not shrink from this responsibility – I welcome it. I do not believe that any of us would exchange places with any other people or any other generation. The energy, the faith, the devotion which we bring to this endeavor will light our country and all who serve it – and the glow from that fire can truly light the world.' Something in the story, something in the times, that had to have been sensed, felt, but never thought out, never shaped into a theory or a belief or even a notion, propelled these people out of themselves, past their limits as artists or actors or technicians, and made them propel their material, Richard Condon's cheaply paranoid fantasy, past its limits.

There's a special thrill that comes when you recognise an author working over his head, over her head – and in *The Manchurian Candidate* everyone, from Frankenheimer to Sinatra to the uncredited extra who flies across the stage in the midst of the carnage at the end of the film, seems like an author. Bob Dylan was not working over his head when in 1965 he made 'Like a Rolling Stone'; he was realising a talent, and a vision, that was implicit in his previous work. The same was true with Aretha Franklin in 1967, when after years of aesthetic suppression, her gospel desires locked up in Columbia albums of supper-club standards, she made her first record on Atlantic, with rhythm and blues producer Jerry Wexler, and stunned the world with 'I Never Loved a Man (The Way I Love You)'. But reading *Uncle Tom's Cabin*, even if you've never read the novels Harriet Beecher Stowe wrote before or after, you can

sense an author driving her story and being driven by it – being driven by her times, by the smallest, most subtle details inherent in every character or setting she's invented, borrowed or stolen: the provenance becomes irrelevant.

Here clichés turn into horrors. The ordinary becomes marvellous. Anything can happen. Even with a screenplay, where the director and the actors are playing out a script, where every moment may be storyboarded, defined, fixed in advance – even here, nothing is fixed in advance. There's no storyboard, no script, no director's instruction, no actor's intention that can call up, that can demand, that can account for the complexity of Major Marco's smile when he finally proves that his dream was not a dream, but a memory – when he begins, finally, to break the case, when he knows that others know that his dream was real. His smile is warm; it is sadistic. It's happy; it's determined, against all odds. As far as Sinatra's character is concerned – as far as Marco sees – the movie can end right here. A whole life, and its future, is in that smile – along with the promise of a happy ending, the happy ending the movie won't provide, the ending that the smile, so all-consuming and complete as it appears on the screen, won't get.

6

. . . .

THE PLEASURE OF ITS VIOLENCE

Those following the proceedings during the past year of the Senate Select Committee on POW and MIA Affairs have been mystified by the rabid actions of the one man on the committee who should be grateful that for nearly three decades there have been activists in America who have refused to let die the issue of the fate of Americans lost and missing in Southeast Asia from the Vietnam War.

I am speaking of course of Sen. John McCain (R-Ariz.). None of the Senators on the Select Committee have been as vicious in their attacks on POW/MIA family members and activists than the man behind the mask of war hero, former POW, and patriotic United States Senator ... Borrowing from the title of a popular movie of some years ago, many activists who have felt the fangs of this pit bull call him the 'Manchurian Candidate.'

Ted Sampley, *US Veteran Dispatch*, December 1992

At an internet start-up in Michigan last week, a voter asked John McCain why he had changed his mind after 1996 and decided to run for president. McCain deadpanned: 'I was sitting in a room and Angela Lansbury turned over a Queen of Diamonds.'

Jonathan Alter, 'The Old Order Closes Ranks', *Newsweek*, 21 February 2000

The plot of *The Manchurian Candidate* is an exploitation of terrors floating in the air in 1959: the terror of McCarthyism, where in the United States any citizen could at any time be called a Communist and then blacklisted, deprived of her job, cast out of his community; the terror of Communist brainwashing, good American boys in Korea tortured with beatings, castor oil, drugs, with unimaginable techniques, until they denounced their own country and praised their own enemies. The Soviets and the Chinese Communists have made an amnesiac assassin out of American soldier Raymond Shaw and contrived to have him awarded the Congressional Medal of Honor, to place him above suspicion, beyond reproach. Their comrade in the United States is Shaw's mother, whose husband is Senator John Iselin, a stand-in for Senator Joe McCarthy.

(Frankenheimer would speak with pride of his job as the assistant director on the episode of '*See It Now* with Edward R. Murrow the night he nailed Senator McCarthy'.) Posing as rabid anti-Communists, Senator and Mrs Iselin are Communist agents. Ultimately, Senator Iselin will win the vice-presidential nomination of his party; his stepson Raymond Shaw is to assassinate the presidential nominee as the nominee delivers his acceptance speech, and then Senator Iselin will take his place with a great patriotic address – 'defending America even if it means his own death', Raymond's mother explains as she gives him his assignment. And then Senator Iselin, or rather his Communist masters, or rather Eleanor Iselin, will be swept into power, which she will exercise as pure sadism, for its own sake, betraying her one-time comrades, destroying them and, the implication is, everything else. The United States. The republic. Herself. All for the pure pleasure of the act – for the pleasure of its violence.

Save as an entry into a certain state of mind, there is no point in pausing over this plot as a clue to anything. The plot, in this movie, is an excuse – an excuse for the pleasure of its violence. That is, you're going to see everything you ever believed was fixed and given suspended in the air and then dashed to the ground. That's a thrill. You're going to believe the notion that a single person could, by means of a single bullet, change history, transform it utterly. Nonsense – even if it happened, in the years after *The Manchurian Candidate* was made, again and again. Historians tell us that it didn't happen; that solitary individuals, even solitary individuals acting out great, historic conspiracies, don't make history. History is made by invisible hands.

As it plays, *The Manchurian Candidate* raises none of these questions. It revels in absurdity, works off it, takes absurdity as a power principle: the power of entertainment. The movie takes absurdity as a pleasure principle: the pleasure of the smallest detail catching the heart of a story in a way that whoever came up with the moment may never have explained even to himself or herself, just found a hunch and played it – Eleanor Iselin appearing at her costume party as Little Bo Peep, unless she's really Marie Antoinette in her milkmaid clothes. The movie – and I can't think of another movie that in its smallest details is so naturalistic and in its overarching tone is so crazy – is first of all fun. It's slapstick, as Pauline Kael said, who loved the film ('I have talked to a number of people about why they hated *The Manchurian Candidate*,' Kael wrote in 1962, 'and I swear not one of them can remember that when the liberal senator is killed, milk pours out'); 'pure jazz,' said Manny Farber, who didn't love it, but who had to be talking about bebop – this movie is not Duke Ellington. You can see this spirit, this heedlessness, this narrative irresponsibility, in a scene that didn't have to be anything more than a transitional device, a counter in the plot.

'Mr Secretary?'
Major Marco's schizophrenic dreams have led him to a near breakdown; the Army has relieved him of his duties as an intelligence officer and reassigned him as a public relations assistant to the secretary of defense. The secretary is holding a press conference, with Marco seated at his side.

'Mr Secretary,' says a reporter, 'can you explain the cut in budget?' The secretary, bulbous and impatient, with a hint of Lyndon Johnson in his vehemence, but with none of Johnson's savvy, explodes. 'Since you've asked a simple-minded question,' he roars, 'I'll give you an equally simple-minded answer.' The secretary goes on to explain, in words so straightforward you can't imagine them being spoken today (and with a logic so straightforward you can't imagine it ever applying to a bureaucracy), that because no naval power threatens the Free World, there is no need to build more ships; thus the cut in budget. We see a room filled up with reporters, cameras, TV monitors – as in Major Marco's dream, the scene is at once whole and all cut up. Now we see the secretary directly, then on a TV monitor, then again directly, then from the crowd, then the room from his point of view, everything moving fast.

The secretary is responding rudely, with great humour. You're caught by a violation – the violation made by plain speech, a violation of all the rules of bureaucratic propriety. Who is this man? How did he get appointed? This is more lively, more real, than government is supposed to be, but it's just a warm-up. As Major Marco tries to end the press conference, Senator Iselin stands up in the back of the room. Eleanor Iselin, sitting well off to the side, is silently mouthing the words Senator Iselin is going to speak, words she's written: the accusation that there are 207 card-carrying Communists in the Defense Department, and that the secretary knows it.

In utter chaos, the camera moves from the secretary to Iselin to a TV monitor fixed on the secretary, the monitor camera then panning – blurring, sliding, ripping – to pick up Iselin again. He speaks from both

The press conference:
montage inside montage

the monitor and in the room – it's a kind of epistemological violence, a set of media contradictions fed into an actual event, or vice versa. But the event is dissolving; even as it proceeds, all that's left of it are its representations. The secretary is beside himself. He doesn't answer Iselin's ridiculous charge; he says, 'Throw that lunatic out of here! You claim to be a senator? Senator of what, I want to know! If this man is ever here again I want him thrown out, *bodily*. Never, do you understand me! NOT *EVER!*'

You lose any real sense of the development of the plot; you're captured by the weird spectacle of a high government official saying exactly what he means. You forget that, of course, the secretary of defense would know who Senator Iselin is. You revel in the secretary's disbelief and refusal. Wouldn't it be wonderful, you think, if our government actually talked like that? That's the pleasure; that's what stays in your mind. In the moment, you don't care about Senator Iselin, about the strange and hideous conspiracy that's unfolding. You want to see the secretary of defense keep talking – you want to see him take over the story. And he does, in a way. Even though we never see him again, his spirit – breaking all the boundaries of what you've come to expect – is what the movie is about: what it's for.

Then and Now

When you look, now, at this 1962 black-and-white movie made up of bits and pieces of Hitchcock and Orson Welles, of *Psycho* and *Citizen Kane* most obviously – perhaps less obviously, but more completely, taking *Invasion of the Body Snatchers* out of science fiction and returning it to history – made up of a lot of clean steals, workmanlike thievery, a second-class director with a first-class cast using whatever he can get his hands on – what's overwhelming is a sense of what the movie does that movies can no longer do. The momentum of the film is so strong you may not catch this dislocation until the second time you see the picture, the third time, the tenth time – but that sense, that itch, may keep calling you back.

I remember first seeing it alone, when it came out in 1962, at the Varsity Theatre in Palo Alto, California, a Moorish wonderland of a movie house. The first thing I did when it was over was call my best friend and tell him he had to see it, too. We went the next night; as we left the theatre, I asked him what he thought. 'Greatest movie I ever saw,' he said flatly, as if he didn't want to talk about it, and he didn't. He said what he said stunned, with bitterness, as if he shouldn't have had to see this thing, as if what it told him was both true and false in a manner he would never be able to untangle, as if it was both incomprehensible and all too clear, as if the whole experience had been, somehow, a gift, the gift of art, and also *unfair* – and that was how I felt, too.

We saw – as anyone can see today – too many rules broken. It's one thing to have Raymond Shaw, the nasty, boring prig, made into an assassin; the zombie state he's put into when he has to kill is not, really, so far from his everyday life. When his controllers make him kill his boss – in 1954, two years after his conditioning in Manchuria, to see if 'the mechanisms', the codes, keys, triggers and responses, are still functioning properly – the manner in which Shaw performs the act is not all that different from the way he speaks or gestures to anyone else he might encounter. But it's something else to see him enter the house of Senator Iselin's sworn enemy – Senator Thomas Jordan, who is, for one day, Raymond Shaw's father-in-law. On orders from his mother, his 'American operator', Raymond shoots the senator, from a distance, through the heart: through the milk carton the senator is holding in front of himself as he stands by his refrigerator in the middle of the night, welcoming his new son-in-law into the family. It's not horrible – in the Castro Theatre in San Francisco in 2001, some in the audience were still laughing as milk spurted from the carton and the senator fell to the floor. In the moment, the action is too direct, unhestitating, too unadorned to

Raymond Shaw, under the Jordan eagle

Two of the dead

be anything but a hole in the story it is advancing. But then Raymond, being careful not to step in the milk on the floor, approaches the body and puts the necessary, professional second shot into the dead man's brain. As he does so, his wife, the senator's daughter, comes running down the stairs in her nightgown, into the frame – and then Raymond, who has been programmed not only to kill his target but to kill any witnesses to any killing, unhesitatingly, without the slightest human response (though he still, somehow, seems to be himself, an actual person), turns and shoots his wife through the forehead. And at this point the audience in the Castro sucked in its breath in a single, audible gasp. You could feel the air go right out of the room.

When the Movie Stops

'We don't take our stories straight any more,' Pauline Kael wrote in 1967, in her famous *New Yorker* review of *Bonnie and Clyde* – her first piece for the magazine, written as an intervention, to save the film from a flood of condemnation by liberal critics appalled by its violence and amorality. 'This isn't necessarily bad,' she went on: '*Bonnie and Clyde* is the first film demonstration that the put-on can be used for the purposes of art. *The Manchurian Candidate* almost succeeded in that, but what was implicitly wild and far-out in the material was nevertheless presented on screen as a straight thriller. *Bonnie and Clyde* keeps the audience in a kind of eager, nervous imbalance – holds our attention by throwing our disbelief back in our faces. To be put on is to be put on the spot, put on the stage, made the stooge in a comedy act. People in the audience at *Bonnie and Clyde* are laughing, demonstrating that they're not stooges – that they appreciate the joke – when they catch the first bullet right in the face.' But it is precisely the straightness of the presentation that allows Raymond Shaw's bullet to hit the audience in the face, and with more force than any shot fired in *Bonnie and Clyde*.

And Laurence Harvey's shot through Leslie Parrish's forehead is not even the worst. At the end of the movie, at the party convention, as Raymond Shaw perches high in Madison Square Garden, hidden in a spotlight booth, positioned to assassinate the presidential nominee – at the end, when Raymond instead shoots his stepfather, Senator Iselin, there is an instant cut to Raymond's mother, seated next to the senator, as she realises what's coming. A second bullet goes through her forehead, and her hands jerk to her head – just as, everyone who has seen the film since 22 November 1963 has to remember, President Kennedy's hands would go to his neck.

By this time we have seen a ruined Raymond Shaw in a filthy hotel room across from the convention site, the headlines in the newspaper in his hand screaming out the deaths of his wife and father-in-law, as he piteously calls Major Marco to ask him what happened. We've seen Sinatra, with a deck of fifty-two Queen of Diamonds cards, crack Raymond's code, until, step by step, death by death, he has taken Raymond through every killing he has done, and we have seen what is left of Raymond when Marco is finished. We have seen Sinatra declare Harvey cured, erased, wiped clean: 'All the Queen's horses and all the Queen's men can never put old Raymond together again.' We have seen Sinatra as Harvey takes a call from 'my American operator', and we have watched

All the Queen's horses, all
the Queen's men

Sinatra's face as it wavers towards surprise and somehow stops short of it as Harvey says, 'Yes, mother.' In Condon's novel, it is here that Marco sends Shaw off to kill the Iselins; in the film, no such thing happens. Marco has cracked the code but not solved the case; neither he nor Shaw knows what Shaw is supposed to do. Neither has yet grasped even the outline of the plot. So Shaw leaves to receive his final instructions from his American operator, with Marco certain that Shaw is now *his* man – his own man. But finally, waiting for the call Shaw is supposed to make, to tell Marco what his operator told him, the call that never comes, Marco realises he has no idea who Raymond Shaw is now, and neither do we. Except that, having seen him confront his own crimes and be ordered by Marco to forget them, we don't believe that he can forget them: that Marco's magic will be, as he will so bitterly put it, 'better than their magic'.

As Raymond goes off to his assignation with his mother, we know that he is carrying images of what he has done in his head as surely as we are carrying them in ours – and thus he is no longer merely a weapon, a 'mechanism', or a prig. We see him as an individual who might possibly have a life to live – and so when he commits the final, necessary, fated, heroic crime, when he kills his mother, in that instant the movie stops. You stop: as you realise what's happened, the horror of every death is doubled. His father-in-law, his wife, his stepfather, his mother, then himself – he has to kill them all. It's right, but you can't cheer, not even inwardly, when Raymond Shaw shoots his mother, the villain. You think: My God, he's killed his mother. What can he do next? He has to kill himself – but that's not the ending you want. And you can't accept it.

Go
This kind of violation, this extremism – presented, for all of its impossibility and absurdism, in a mode of naturalism, and the naturalism sealed by the believability of each smile, each fast reach for a hat, every expression and every gesture – is not all there is in *The Manchurian Candidate* that is not in movies today. There is that sense of people working over their heads, which is really a sense of playfulness: What can we get away with? What will people catch? What's going to go right past them? Do we really care?

Do we care that the disaster building inside the film is present even before it begins, in David Amram's title theme? The theme is reminiscent, now, of Nino Rota's theme for *The Godfather*, but what makes it different is the absence of stateliness – of power. Instead, before anything has happened, there is a fatal undercurrent of sadness, of regret for things lost that can never be recovered, for acts committed that can never be undone, and the pull of the music is as great as it is in Hank Williams's posthumously released 1949 recording 'Alone and Forsaken', which the composer John Fahey called 'the greatest song of despair ever written', which it is. 'We met in the springtime,' the song begins; 'By the fifth word,' Fahey wrote, 'you know it's all over,' and the same is true no farther into Amram's melody.

What about all that stuff Dick Sylbert's doing? We don't want anyone to notice the fabulous clutter in the Army Intelligence room, the grime in the police station, the old wood of Senator Jordan's country house, you're not supposed to notice realism like that – it's just supposed to make everything *else* we're doing seem real. But even all the way back in their minds, will people catch what Sylbert did when he put eagle's wings in both of Tom Jordan's houses, giving him his own special patriotic symbol, and had us put John McGiver right in front of it, so that when he speaks the wings look like they're coming right out of his head? Will anyone know that doesn't just mean Tom Jordan embodies the republic, but that he's doomed, because Dick re-created one of those Puritan gravestones you see all over Massachusetts, with angels' wings coming out of a skull?

Do we care if they get the Lincoln theme – and what is the Lincoln theme, anyway? How did so much Railsplitter stuff get into this picture? How did *that* start? Was it you, George? You, John? Did Sylbert pick up on something in the script, and before we knew it it was everywhere? Let's see, first there's that shot of Jimmy Gregory, Senator Iselin in his DC house in his bathrobe reflected in the glass covering a huge portrait of the Great Emancipator – that's sort of a good joke, but the shot is framed so elegantly it's as if it's true history and not a joke at all. Then there's the other Lincoln portrait in the Iselins' country house on the lake, watching as Angela denounces Tom Jordan, 'This man is evil, this man stands for evil' – don't you love the way she says it, *eve-il*? And in the same scene, that incredible lamp framing her as she speaks, with a bust of Lincoln for the base and the shade in the shape of a stovepipe hat? What Vermont antique store did Sylbert find *that* in? Then there's Iselin dressed up as Lincoln at the costume party, of course – he has to take off the hat to do the limbo, falling on his face drunk – then the Iselin supporters at the convention, dressed just like he is at the party, in their hats and fake

56 'It was as if he had not only forseen the drama but had even seen all around it': Senator Thomas Jordan (John McGiver, top); Eleanor Iselin waits for Raymond Shaw (middle); Senator John Iselin (James Gregory) in Washington, D.C. (bottom)

The Iselin study (top); Senators Jordan and Iselin at the Iselin party (middle); Raymond Shaw, Eleanor Iselin and their shadow (bottom)

beards. But even more than that, it's the scene in the study in the Iselin house. That's when Angela says to Larry Harvey, right out of the blue – the audience will know it's coming and at the same time they won't – 'Raymond, why don't you pass the time by playing a little solitaire?' It's the way the camera moves into the study for that scene, panning across the room but picking up the large bust of Lincoln before anything else comes into focus: it's looking you right in the face, or it would be, if Lincoln's eyes weren't cast down, as if there's something in this room he can't bear to look at. There's the smaller bust of Lincoln on the desk in the same shot that you see as Angela starts speaking – and that's it, that's why Lincoln's in the scene. He *can't* speak. This is the Lincoln Edmund Wilson wrote about – did you ever read that, from *Patriotic Gore*? Wilson writing with such sorrow and awe you can feel his fingers shaking? Lincoln at the end, the republic saved, but one last act to come? 'It was as if he had not only forseen the drama but had even seen all around it … In the poem that Lincoln lived, Booth had been prepared for, too, and the tragic conclusion was necessary to justify all the rest. It was dramatically and morally inevitable that this prophet who had overruled opposition and sent thousands of men to their deaths should finally attest his good faith by laying down his own life with theirs.'

That's the Lincoln who's in the Iselin study, that sorrow and awe at who he was and what he did is what his face is *made* of, but now he's here as a witness, as mute, as powerless as we'd be – he's there *as* the audience. He's there to be forced to witness the plot to destroy the republic he preserved.

Go, Go

What can we get away with? That's what's happening with the casting of a black actor, Joe Adams, to play the Army psychiatrist – one of the few completely sympathetic characters in the film, along with Sinatra's Major Marco and Khigh Dhiegh's Yen Lo – Yen Lo, always a joker, a regular guy, someone you'd love to go out to dinner with. Here we are, in 1962, and a black man is playing a professional, a thinker, and it's not commented on, it's not an issue, but it's still a shock. The man is just doing his job, and no one pays it any mind. How many other American movies use a black actor to play what audiences expect to be a white character without even bothering to point it out, to pat themselves on the back, to congratulate themselves? Adams's psychiatrist is always cool,

The Army psychiatrist
(Joe Adams)

smooth, *suave*, with a cutting sense of humour and a smile on his face that never breaks – and you can imagine it's only Adams, as a foil, who brings out the hipster in Sinatra, as Sinatra tells the psychiatrist that he knows what Raymond Shaw was doing with his hands in that New Jersey hotel in Manchuria, automatically laying out the invisible cards on the table before him: 'I remember – I *remember*. I can see that Chinese cat standing there like Fu Manchu and saying, "The Queen of Diamonds is reminiscent in many ways of Raymond's dearly loved and hated mother …" *Yeeaaahhhh*,' Sinatra's Major Marco says, just like a man rolling a seven all the way down the table. In a way, Adams's psychiatrist is as displacing as Raymond Shaw's murder of his mother. And that's people working over their heads: Let's do it! Let's mix it up! Who cares!

Finally, though, there is another dimension to *The Manchurian Candidate* that is part of this displacement – not, one might think, part of the glee with which those who made the movie made it, not part of the glee with which they let it happen, played it out, but a dimension that confronts us now, four decades later. That is, we are watching a movie made in another world – and we don't know if the ugly knowledge we bring to the movie is knowledge the movie had or not.

7

. . . .

IN 2000

Up on the podium, the man-who-would-be-president, George Bush the Younger, played his part perfectly, smiling for the camera when it was called for, acting tough on cue, gazing off into the distance looking for a vision, searching diligently for those 'thousand points of light' from that 'shining city on a hill.' Suddenly, I found myself remembering an old, grainy, black-and-white movie – and a long ago, nearly forgotten warning that's as prescient today as it was four decades hence. …

Who's been the real hypnotically-programmed, brainwashed lackey over the past few decades? Was Bush, Sr., placed there to make sure that the dummy Reagan stayed on script? Is Cheney there to make sure Bush, Jr., does the same?

Jerry Klein, 'The New Manchurian Candidate', *Creative Loafing*, 12 August 2000

Ni hao (whaaaaatsuuuuup) Comrade Al Gore Litagator. Jiancha wanle ma? (are you done with your inspection yet?) Albert, would you care for a game of solitaire?

As I watched you give your cute little press conferences about 'every vote counting,' I thought about that great movie, The Manchurian Candidate. You looked suprisingly like Raymond, the brainwashed twad of a man even though you were the candidate of your pals, the communists, socialists, and wealth redistributors. Yes, those pesky Democrats.

Xie xie tongzhi (thanks dude).

Kirk Smith, *Inflyovercountry*, 2000

There are obvious moments that take us out of our time, as we watch the movie today, moments that seal the movie as a curiosity, as a relic, that take place around the edges of the action. There's the glimpse of the elevator operator in Raymond Shaw's apartment building, who smokes in the elevator. Far more than the sight of late-1950s, early-1960s cars on the screen, or the use of the Korean War as a social fact it's assumed everyone understands, or Joe McCarthy as a monster or a hero everyone only recently applauded or reviled, this is odd. We know that elevator operators, to the degree that they even exist, can't do that any more. We know that even if we get another Korean War, another Joe McCarthy, we won't get any more elevator operators smoking in elevators. Such tiny details, as we see them today, make the movie seem safe. They protect us from it. Maybe, subliminally, as the movie plays itself out, we try to hold onto such details, because the rest of the movie is too familiar.

The Manchurian Candidate, plunging towards the assassination of a would-be president, climaxing with the assassination of the man who's going to take his place, was taken out of circulation not long after it was released. Not that quickly, not right after the assassination of President Kennedy; while Frankenheimer refused to allow a second theatrical run, the film played on television. Then it went missing. Certainly among those who remembered it, as year after year people continued to tell others about it, about how they had to see it, only to discover that they couldn't, there was a feeling that the film might be part of the inexplicable cycle of assassinations that followed it – a feeling that went far beyond anything in, say, Richard Condon's '"Manchurian Candidate" in Dallas', published in the 28 December 1963 number of the *Nation*: 'I was reading about how Senator Thurston Morton of Kentucky absolved the American people from any guilt in the assassination of the President when a reporter from a South African press association telephoned from London to ask if I felt responsible for the President's killing, inasmuch as I had written a novel, *The Manchurian Candidate*, on which had been based a film that had just been "frozen" in the United States because it was felt that the assassin might have seen it and been influenced by it. I told the reporter that, with all Americans, I had contributed to form the attitudes of the assassin; and that the assassin, and Americans like him, had contributed to the attitudes which had caused me to write the novel.' Rather it was a feeling that the film was part of the supposedly scattered but obviously whole, complete, singular event that the cycle of assassinations comprised: its transformation of what in the United States had been taken as open, public life into private crime or hidden conspiracy. And there must have been a feeling, as the film itself stayed hidden, that the country's real history, history as it is lived out every day, its fundamental premises of work and leisure, love and death, might be a kind of awful secret that no one would ever understand.

As the movie ends, in its final scene, Sinatra's Marco understands the whole story – why it happened, how it happened – and he can't accept it. 'Hell,' he curses. 'Hell.' That's the end of the film: misery, regret, fury, the secret he has to hold inside himself. It can't be told, that the Soviet Union and the People's Republic of China conspired with purported American anti-Communists, who linked themselves with fascist tendencies in American life, in order to destroy the American republic. The repercussions would be too great. Marco will have to take the secret to his grave. The truth of the life and near death of the republic cannot be told to the people who are the republic. It will be buried, for our own good.

So you look at the movie, lost in its visual delights, cringing at its violence, wondering what it says, if it says anything, weighed down by the knowledge you bring to it, freed from that knowledge by those moments in the film that are unburdened by any moral weight at all – such as the great karate fight between Sinatra's Marco and Henry Silva's Chunjin. In 1962, no one had seen anything like it – and while audiences today, schooled on Bruce Lee and Hong Kong cinema, find the fight clumsy and laugh, it retains a desperation the infinitely more brilliant, stylised bouts that followed don't hint at, because those fights are about themselves, their own reward, and this fight was not.

An Instinctive Act

Chunjin has been sent to New York to watch over Raymond Shaw; he has inveigled himself into Shaw's life as his houseboy. Sinatra, just beginning his quest to understand his dreams, rings the doorbell to Shaw's apartment, hoping for answers. Silva opens the door, Sinatra sees Silva, the whole betrayal in Korea comes back to him, as a fact, still incomprehensible but undeniable, and Sinatra slams Silva in the face. After the fight has gone on, and on, not a second too long, there is a moment when Sinatra has Silva down on the floor, is kicking him in the ribs, again and again, each movement as precise as it is fierce, with each kick Sinatra asking Silva what happened in Korea, what *really* happened, *What was Raymond doing with his hands?* – and then the cops arrive and Sinatra, not thinking in the present but acting in the real world, responds to a cop grabbing his shoulder by elbowing the man in the stomach, and the cop falls away, and the scene is cut. It's a purely instinctive act – and it sums up so much of what's alive about the film.

Marco sees Chunjin
(Henry Silva); Chunjin
sees Marco

But that is not all. After so many years, or after you see the movie now, more than once, another element enters. You see that, here, everyone acts politically: the villains, the heroes, the characters that barely register, those who simply come and go. Everyone acts as a citizen of the republic, or as an anticitizen. What's at stake is a commonwealth. As the movie closes, in that final scene, Major Marco rewrites the dead Raymond Shaw's Medal of Honor citation. In 1952, in what, now, seems so long ago, it had been a conditioned Marco himself who had recommended Shaw for the posting: 'He saved our lives,' as Marco had said, parroting his lines for Yen Lo in Manchuria, 'and took out a complete company of Chinese infantry.' 'Made,' Marco says now, with a long pause, the words not coming easily, 'to commit acts – too unspeakable to be cited here. He freed himself, and in the end, heroically and unhestitatingly, gave his life to save his country.'

The words carry enormous weight – the weight of the idea of one's country, one's community, one's social identity. Of course, this is no less an absurdity, no less a fantasy, than anything else in *The Manchurian Candidate*: the idea that a single person could ruin the commonwealth, or save it. That is where all the folkore of the movie comes from, all the constant twists and turns of the catchphrase 'Manchurian Candidate' as it has entered our language and so easily summed up moments in history that cannot be summed up – where the folklore comes from, and where it stays. But the film has, perhaps without intention, played against this idea of the single, all-powerful hero, or all-powerful villain, throughout its length. In this movie, everyone, hero or villain, minor character and star, has appeared not as a function of the plot, but as someone who acts as if the life of the republic depended on his or her actions, on his or her convictions, beliefs, his or her will, motive, desire.

Pay Any Price
In 2000, as part of an undergraduate seminar at Princeton called 'Prophecy and the American Voice', I screened a video of *The Manchurian Candidate*. The reading for that week was John F. Kennedy's Inaugural Address. Nearly forty years after, it remained threatening – but so full of apparent idealism that that strain was muted. The Cuban Missile Crisis of 1962, and the stated will to engage in nuclear war to resolve it, were already present on 20 January 1961: 'We shall pay any price, bear any burden, meet any hardship, support any friend, oppose any foe, in order to assure the survival and success of liberty.' It was only an echo of Winston Churchill's Address to the House of Commons on 4 June 1940 – 'We shall defend our island, whatever the cost may be, we shall fight on the beaches, we shall fight on the landing grounds, we shall fight in the fields and in the streets, we shall fight in the hills, we shall never surrender' – but Kennedy made the prospect sound more exciting than terrifying, and his words stirred the nation.

I had paired Kennedy's speech with the film because of a sense that for all of Kennedy's call to glory, to nobility, to a mission bigger and finer than any individual who felt called to it – and most who made *The Manchurian Candidate*, one can be sure, had, if only for a moment, felt called to it – there was in the movie an apprehension that everything was out of joint. There was a felt, even thrilled embrace of the notion that nothing was what it seemed, that some terrible conspiracy, some terrible betrayal was at work – and there was. In the White House, Kennedy was continuing his affair with a woman to whom he had been introduced by Frank Sinatra: Judith Campbell, who was simultaneously carrying on an affair with Sam Giancana, head of the Chicago mob. While the country was rededicating itself to the New Frontier, the administration was working with the mafia in Chicago and New Orleans to assassinate Fidel Castro; a more classic conspiracy could not be imagined. When Lyndon Johnson became president he found he had been cut out of Cuban policy-making; 'We were running a goddamned Murder, Inc., in the Caribbean,' he later said. Johnson believed Castro had Kennedy killed because Kennedy had tried to kill him.

In my class, before I ran the film, I played a cassette I'd made up one afternoon the year before. Playing various end-of-an-era retrospective CDs, I'd found myself in the midst of an accidental, self-generating collage of what seemed to be the whole of the world sensed, feared, or even wished for in *The Manchurian Candidate* – but not anticipated, predicted, or even hinted at as any kind of warning, to make any kind of point. Listening, I felt as if I were seeing the move from the inside – having lived on past its moment and through its future. Pieces of the collage came together over the hours, as one set of CDs led to another – the two discs of *I Can Hear It Now/The Sixties*, by Fred W. Friendly and Walter Cronkite, the fifteen discs of *The Century*, by Peter Jennings and Todd Brewster. Each piece was like a clue, driving backwards or forwards to the next one, until finally it was as if they had all been programmed together, one after the other, and everything else on the discs fell away. This, I said to the class before I played the tape, was what the political culture of the years that preceded and followed the release of *The Manchurian Candidate* was like; this is how it felt.

First there was Frank Sinatra in 1960, in a rewrite of his 1959 children's-song hit, 'High Hopes', now a Kennedy campaign theme: 'Everyone is voting for Jack/ 'Cause he's got what all the rest lack,' Sinatra sang flatly, with horns behind him, then hitting the chorus that was everywhere in that election season: 'Everyone wants to/ BACK/ JACK/ Jack is on the right track.' And then, recorded much later, Janet Leigh – and if not because of the movie, why Janet Leigh? 'His enthusiasm, his, *energy*, and *determination*, it was, *infectious*. And we all felt – and the *country felt* – that, *yes!* you know, we're *on the march again*, and it was a *good* march.' And then Ron Jenkins of radio station KBOX in Dallas.

'Hello?' you hear as if from a distance – a faint signal, the reporter trying to establish contact. Then: 'It, it appears as if something has happened in the motorcade route, something, I repeat, has happened, in the motorcade route. There's numerous people running up, the, hill – alongside Elm Street, there by the Simmons Freeway, several police officers are rushing, up the hill at this time, stand by, just a moment please. Something has happened in the motorcade route. Stand by please.' He is holding onto his voice. Then he's not. 'PUT ME ON, PHIL, PUT ME ON!' Desperately: '*Phil, am I on?*' He takes a breath: 'We're here at the Trademart, *the motorcade is coming by here, I can see many many motorcycles coming by now,* police motorcycles – just heard a call on the radio for *all units* along Industrial, to pick up the motorcade, something has happened here, we understand there has been a shooting, the presidential car coming up now, we know it's the presidential car, I can see Mrs Kennedy' – and here a huge siren sound winds around every word from the reporter like a rope – 'in her pink suit, there's a Secret Service man spread-eagled over the top of the car' – and the sirens multiply – 'we understand Governor and Mrs Connally are in the car with President and Mrs Kennedy' – the sirens now seem to be driving the motorcade, you can feel it moving past the reporter like a flood –'we can't see who has been hit if anybody's been hit, but apparently something is wrong here, something is terribly wrong. I'm in behind the motorcade – it looks as though they're going to Parkland Hospital, we're on the road to Parkland at this time—' The sirens fade. It's as if you are in the moment; as if you still don't know what happened.

'Here he comes,' someone says two days later; then Ike Pappas of WNEW of New York is speaking. 'Now the prisoner, uh, wearing a black sweater—' Pappas's voice is controlled, but you can almost feel it shaking, as if the ground is moving under the reporter's feet. 'He has changed, from his T-shirt, is being moved out toward' – and there's a shudder in Pappas's voice now, as if something is about to happen – '*an armoured car.*' Now steady again: 'Being led out by, uh, Captain Fritz' – there is the long honk of an automobile horn. 'There is the prisoner,' and Pappas addresses him: 'Do you have anything to say in your defence—' and as soon as the last word is out of his mouth there is the overwhelmingly powerful report of a firearm. 'AHHH!' someone cries. 'UHHHH!' 'He's been shot,' someone says. 'THERE'S A SHOT!' Pappas says. 'Oswald has been shot!' He sounds as if he is no more than a foot away, and if he's holding the event in his hands, trying to keep it from spilling to the floor. There is the sound of commotion. Pappas's voice takes on a hard, gritty edge: 'Oswald has been shot ... *Holy mackerel* ... a shot rang out as he was led' – and Pappas is losing his breath – 'into his car.' Pappas sounds as if he's being carried forward by a crowd even as he falls behind it, as the shouts around him grow dimmer: 'There's a mass confusion, uh, rolling in the—' It's the sound of everything breaking, everything falling apart, of too much happening too fast, the event, history itself, getting away from the words chasing it: 'Fighting,' and Pappas is fighting for every breath, 'uh, uh, as he was being led out now he's being—' It's almost unbearable to listen to. A vortex has opened up in the century and the reporter is hanging onto its edges with his fingernails. 'Led back he was, thrown to the ground, the police have the entire area blocked off, "Everybody stay back," is the yell,' and now suddenly Pappas is shockingly authoritative, for a moment merely descriptive: 'Here is the ambulance.' Then he is desperate again: 'He is, being hustled in – to me he appears dead, there is a gunshot wound in his lower abdomen. He is, *unconscious*' – 'Get the fuck out of the way' someone shouts – 'His hand is dangling, over, the edge of the stretcher, now he's off to the hospital, Parkland Hospital, we believe.' 'Oh, God,' someone says. 'Here are some police officials,' Pappas says, as if to introduce them at a community event. 'Who is he?' 'Jack Ruby is the name,' a man says tiredly. 'Jack Ruby?' 'Jack Ruby. Carousel Club.' 'He runs the Carousel Club?'

'Mr Humphrey has been backgrounding you as far as the delegate votes go,' Andrew West of KRKD in Los Angeles says to Senator Robert F. Kennedy in a harrumphing reporter's voice. They're in the Ambassador Hotel on 5 June 1968; Kennedy has just defeated Senator Eugene McCarthy in the California Democratic presidential primary. 'We'll just have to go back, struggle for it,' Kennedy says in his odd, thin voice. There is an unbelievably fast whooshing sound, like a tape splice, like the air going out of a balloon: 'Senator Kennedy has been' – there are women screaming in fury and terror – 'Senator Kennedy has been shot, is that possible? Is that possible?' 'Get out of—' screams a young man in a commanding voice, a voice that, given what the listener now knows is happening, sounds self-important and stupid. 'Hold everybody!' someone else shouts. 'Hold him back!' 'Ladies and gentlemen, it is possible,' West says, his voice breaking into pieces on the last three words. There are screams everywhere, as if the shooting is still going on. 'Not only Senator Kennedy – *oh, my God* – Senator Kennedy has been shot – *and another man* – a Kennedy campaign manager – and possibly shot, in the head—' The constant screaming from every direction makes it feel as if the room is spinning. 'I am right here, Rafer Johnson has a hold of a man, who apparently' – a woman's hysterical voice almost forms words as she rushes past – 'has fired the shot. *He has fired the shot*, he still has the gun! The gun is pointed at me right at this moment, I hope they can get the gun out of his hands. *Be very careful*,' West says, speaking now from inside the event, from inside history as it is being made, 'GET THE GUN! Get the gun. *Get the gun*. Stay away from the gun!' The room is turning upside down. 'Stay away from the gun. HIS HAND IS FROZEN! *TAKE A HOLD OF HIS THUMB AND BREAK IT IF YOU HAVE TO!* GET HIS THUMB! ALRIGHT – *THAT'S IT, RAFER, GET IT! GET THE GUN, RAFER! HOLD HIM, HOLD HIM*, hold him … We don't want another Oswald.' 'We don't want another Oswald,' a faraway voice echoes West's. The tape stops; the story goes back to the ether.

In 1995

It was at a party at John Frankenheimer's house in Malibu, California, just before the California primary, that the novelist Romain Gary approached Robert Kennedy and said, 'You know, don't you, that somebody is going to kill you?' Frankenheimer had spent 102 days on the campaign with Kennedy, filming speeches and appearances and making advertisements; on the day of the California primary Kennedy decided he wanted to watch the returns at Frankenheimer's house in Malibu. The campaign staff insisted Kennedy be at the Ambassador Hotel for a network interview. Frankenheimer drove him. 'He went in and did the telecast,' Frankenheimer recalled in 1995, speaking to Charles Champlin, but Kennedy nevertheless insisted on returning to Frankenheimer's house as soon as he was able to make his victory speech. Eugene McCarthy was refusing to concede; finally he did. 'Bobby said, "I want you standing next to me on the podium,"' Frankenheimer said. 'I said, "Bobby, I don't think it looks good for you to have a Hollywood director standing next to you. It's not the image." He said, "You're right." And the man who stood next to him was shot, too. That would have been me.'

'Bobby said, "When I say, 'Let's win it in Chicago,' go and get the car. I'll come right out." I was standing there in an archway, feeling like someone in *The Manchurian Candidate*,' Frankenheimer said; as in the scene in his own movie set in the briefing room used by the secretary of defense, he found the action taking place both in the flesh and on TV screens. 'I can see Bobby's face on a big television monitor in the ballroom and I can see his back for real. As I stood there a figure went by me and it was as if there was electricity coming out of his body. I've never felt anything like it before or since. Of course it was Sirhan Sirhan.'

Frankenheimer waited; then came the last act. 'When Bobby said "Let's win it in Chicago," I left and got the Rolls and brought it to the entrance. The next thing I knew there were policemen banging on the car and saying, "Move it!" I said, "This is Senator Kennedy's car." They shouted, "Move it," then a black woman ran out of the hotel shouting, "Kennedy's been shot!" The cops starting hitting the car with their batons. It had to be repainted later. I drove off and turned on the radio and got a CBS flash which said, "Senator Robert Kennedy, his brother-in-law Stephen Smith and movie director John Frankenheimer have been shot."'

8

. . . .

REMEMBERING THE FUTURE

[T]he head of the Psychology Department at Colgate University, George 'Esty' Estabrooks … acknowledged that hypnosis did not work on everyone and that only one person in five made a good enough subject to be placed in a deep trance, or a state of somnabulism. He believed that only these subjects could be induced to do such things against their apparent will as reveal secrets or commit crimes. He had watched respected members of the community make fools of themselves in the hands of stage hypnotists, and he had compelled his own students to reveal fraternity secrets and the details of private love affairs – all of which the students presumably did not want to do.

Still his experience was limited. Estabrooks realised that the only certain way to know whether a person would commit a crime like murder under hypnosis was to have the person kill someone. Unwilling to settle the issue on his own by trying the experiment, he felt that government sanction of the process would relieve the hypnotist of personal responsibility. 'Any "accidents" that might occur during the experiments will be simply charged to profit and loss,' he wrote, 'a very trifling portion of that enormous wastage in human life which is part and parcel of war.'

John Marks, *The Search for the Manchurian Candidate: The CIA and Mind Control* (Times Books, 1979)

On United's first day of flying after the attacks the movies showing were: 'Shrek,' 'Crocodile Dundee,' 'A Knight's Tale' and 'The Manchurian Candidate.' Can you believe that? I was too afraid to watch it.

E-mail report on United Airlines Flight 522 from Chicago to Buenos Aires, 16 September 2001

It all goes back to Major Marco's dream. 'A bad dream,' as Rod Serling asked at the close of a *Twilight Zone* rerun I caught in 1999, when publicity over the turn of the century was reaching its height (guy wakes up, no one recognises him, he's going nuts, he wakes up again, everything's okay, then he stares in horror at the wife he's never seen before), 'or the end of the world?' A cool thing to say in 1962, when the episode first ran. In 1999 it felt like a prophecy – or, as the novelist Steve Erickson defined a dream in *The Sea Came in at Midnight*, which appeared that same year, 'a memory of the future'.

Erickson's novel begins with 1,999 female cultists walking off a cliff in California 'in the last moments of the Twentieth Century', and then introduces both 'the long-lost member of the Shangri-Las' ('expelled from the group before their first hit record for the one night she went down on an entire college fraternity') and 'the Western World's foremost apocalyptologist' (who has determined that the new millennium began not on 31 December 1999 but 'at exactly 3:02 in the morning on the seventh of May, in the year 1968'). The world changed, the apocalyptologist explains – crossed over – when any discernible rationale behind great public events was replaced by a disembodied force of pure perversity. It was a force that reached its 'true vortex' in Year 18 of the apocalyptologist's new calendar, with 'two abysmal events so beyond the pale of unreason that a civilized person could barely bring himself to contemplate them'.

'One, on 5 May 1985, was the pilgrimage of an American president to a German cemetery for the express purpose of laying a wreath in honor of the most singularly vicious, sadistic, and incontestably evil human beings of the twentieth century. The other, only twelve days before on 23 April, was the utterly arbitrary decision by America's greatest soft-drink company to immediately discontinue the single most successful product in the history of modern commerce, in order to produce in its place a bad imitation of its obviously inferior competitor.'

Which is to say that, in Erickson's hands, this is the way our world ended: not with a bang, or a whimper, but with Ronald Reagan, Bitburg, and New Coke.

Prophecy

It's not that *The Manchurian Candidate* prefigured, let alone prophesied, the events that followed it. It didn't. It is a fantasy in which Joe McCarthy, as Thomas Jordan says to Eleanor Iselin of her husband, 'could not do more harm to this country if he were a paid Soviet agent' – a cheap irony, like the folklore that has grown up around the picture, boiling it down to a catchphrase, as Richard Condon himself did from the beginning.

Ben Marco waits with his commanding officer (Douglas Henderson) in the Army Intelligence
office (top); Raymond Shaw waits in the spotlight booth in Madison Square Garden (middle);
Marco's commanding officer waits with Marco (bottom)

74   The Iselins wait in Madison Square Garden; Ben Marco waits in the Garden (middle); Shaw waits (bottom)

What *The Manchurian Candidate* did prefigure – what it acted out, what it played out, in advance – was the state of mind that would accompany the assassinations that followed it, those violations of American public life. It prefigured the sense that the events that shape our lives take place in a world we cannot see, to which we have no access, that we will never be able to explain. If a dream is a memory of the future, this is the future *The Manchurian Candidate* remembered.

Silence

In the classroom at Princeton, the film, projected on a big screen by first-class equipment, was almost over – in Madison Square Garden, the candidates assembled on stage while Laurence Harvey fitted the pieces of his sniper's rifle together and Frank Sinatra raced up the stairs to Harvey's spotlight booth – when the projector broke. The media cabinet in the classroom included a tiny TV monitor; there, the video was still running. Twenty people crowded into a narrow space between the wall and the table bolted to the floor to watch. Nobody moved. It seemed nobody breathed. Everybody was terrified of what would happen next – or that the monitor, too, would break, and they wouldn't find out. Then the Frank Sinatra who had smiled so deeply as he broke the case turned into a man almost dead with sorrow and guilt, reading his epitaph for Raymond Shaw, saying 'Hell … hell.' And then like the first Lincoln bust in the film he looked down, away from himself, as if he could not bear to look at himself, and the movie was over.

We walked out of the room together, no one with a word to say to anyone about anything.

CREDITS

· ·

The Manchurian Candidate

USA
1962

Directed by
John Frankenheimer
Produced by
George Axelrod, John
Frankenheimer
Screenplay by
George Axelrod
Based upon a novel by
Richard Condon
Director of Photography
Lionel Lindon
Film Editor
Ferris Webster
Production Designer
Richard Sylbert
**Music Composed and
Conducted by**
David Amram

©M.C. Productions
Production Company
Released thru United Artists
Executive Producer
Howard W. Koch
Production Assistant
Gene Martell
Assistant Director
Joseph Behm
2nd Assistant Directors
David Salven, Read Killgore
Script Supervisor
Amalia Wade
**Additional Script
Supervisors**
Molly Kent, Grace Dubray
Photographic Effects
Howard Anderson Co.
Operative Cameraman
John Mehl
Camera Assistants
Felix Barlow, Eugene Levitt
Grips
Richard Borland,
Gaylin Schultz

Gaffer
Robert Campbell
Stills
Bill Creamer
Special Effects
Paul Pollard
Assistant Film Editor
Carl Mahakian
Assistant Art Director
Philip M. Jefferies
Set Designers
Lucius O. Croxton,
Seymour Klate,
John M. Elliott,
Joseph S. Tolsby
Set Decorator
George R. Nelson
Property Master
Arden Cripe
Props
Richard M. Rubin
**Maps Provided through
the Courtesy of**
American Map Company,
Inc.
Costumes by
Moss Mabry
Costumer
Wesley V. Jefferies
Wardrobe
Morris Brown, Ron Talsky,
Angela Alexander,
Rose Viebeck
Jewels by
Ruser –Beverly Hills
Make-up Artists
Bernard Ponedel, Jack
Freeman, Ron Berkeley
Additional Make-up
Dorothy Parkinson
Hair Stylist
Mary Westmoreland
**Janet Leigh's Hair Styles
by**
Gene Shacove
Music Editor
Richard Carruth
Music Recording
Vinton Vernon

Sound Mixer
Joe Edmondson
Sound Recording
Paul Wolfe
Boom Operator
William Flannery
Re-recording
Buddy Myers
Sound Effects Editor
Del Harris
Dialogue Coach
Thom Conroy

Cast
Frank Sinatra
Major Bennet Marco
Laurence Harvey
Staff Sergeant Raymond
Shaw
Janet Leigh
Eugénie Rose 'Rosie'
Cheyney
Angela Lansbury
Eleanor Shaw Iselin,
Raymond's mother
Henry Silva
Chunjin
James Gregory
Senator John Yerkes Iselin
Leslie Parrish
Jocelyn 'Jocie' Jordan
John McGiver
Senator Thomas Jordan
Khigh Dhiegh
Yen Lo
James Edwards
Corporal Al Melvin
Douglas Henderson
colonel
Albert Paulsen
Zilkov
Barry Kelley
Secretary of Defense
Lloyd Corrigan
Holborn Gaines
Madame Spivy
Berezovo's lady counterpart

[*uncredited*]
Miyoshi Jingu
Korean girl
Harry Holcombe
general at airport
Helen Kleeb
1st chairlady
Richard LaPore
Ed Navole
Tom Lowell
Bobby Lembeck
John Laurence
Gossfeld
Nicky Blair
Silvers
William Thourlby
Little
Irving Steinberg
Freeman
John Francis
Haiken
Reggie Nalder
Dmitri Gomel
Bess Flowers
Gomel's lady counterpart
Nick Bolin

Berezovo
Whit Bissell
medical officer
Joe Adams
psychiatrist
Mimi Dillard
Mrs Melvin
Maye Henderson
2nd chairlady
Jean Vaughn
nurse
Robert Riordan
Benjamin K. Arthur,
the nominee
Robert Burton
convention chairman
Anton Van Stralen
officer
Mickey Finn
Richard Norris
John Indrisano
reporters
Lou Krugg
manager
Mike Masters
Tom Harris
FBI men
Mariquita Moll
soprano
Karen Norris
secretary
Ray Spiker
policeman
Merritt Bohn
Jilly
Frank Basso
photographer
Julie Payne
Lana Crawford
Evelyn Byrd
guests at party

Estelle Etterre
Mary Benoit
Rita Kenaston
Maggie Hathaway
Joan Douglas
Frances Nealy
Evelyn Byrd
women in hotel lobby
Ralph Gambina
Sam 'Kid' Hogan
men in hotel lobby
James Yagi
Lee Tung Foo
Raynum Tsukamoto
Chinese gentlemen in hotel
lobby

11,352 feet
126 minutes

Black and White

Credits compiled by
Markku Salmi,
BFI Filmographic Unit

SOURCES

. . . .

Amram, David, *The Manchurian Candidate –
Complete Soundtrack Recording* (Premier
CD, 1962/1997).

Clark, T. J., *Farewell to an Idea: Episodes from a
History of Modernism* (New Haven and
London: Yale Univesity Press, 1999).

Condon, Richard, *The Manchurian Candidate*
(1959; New York: Jove, 1988).

Cronkite, Walter (narrator), *I Can Hear It
Now/The Sixties*, written and edited by
Fred Friendly and Walker Cronkite
(Columbia Legacy CD set, 1999).

Erickson, Steve, *The Sea Came in at Midnight*
(New York: Bard/Avon, 1999).

Fahey, John, 'The Center of Interest Will Not
Hold', in *How Bluegrass Music Destroyed
My Life* (Chicago: Drag City, 2000).

Frankenheimer, John, *John Frankenheimer: A
Conversation*. With Charles Champlin
(Burbank, CA: Directors Guild of
America/Riverside, 1995).

Jennings, Peter and Todd Brewster, *The
Century* ('Poisoned Dreams, 1960–1963',
#10), (BDD Audio CD set, 1998).

Kael, Pauline, 'Bonnie and Clyde' (1967), in
Kiss Kiss Bang Bang (Boston: Atlantic
Monthly Press/Little, Brown, 1968).

Melville, Herman, Letter to Nathaniel
Hawthorne (17 [?] November 1851), in *The
Portable Melville* (1952), edited by Jay
Leyda (New York: Viking, 1967).

Sinatra, Frank, John Frankenheimer and
George Axelrod, Interview included with
video release of *The Manchurian Candidate*
(MGM/UA Home Video, 1988).

Williams, Hank, 'Alone and Forsaken' (1949),
on *Alone and Forsaken* (Mercury CD, 1995)
or *The Complete Hank Williams* (Mercury
CD set, #7, 1998).

Wilson, Edmund, 'Abraham Lincoln', in
*Patriotic Gore: Studies in the Literature the
American Civil War* (New York: Oxford
University Press, 1962). First published in
different form as 'Abraham Lincoln: The
Union as Religious Mysticism' (1953) in
Eight Essays (Garden City, NY:
Doubleday Anchor, 1954).

ALSO PUBLISHED

If you would like further information about future BFI Film Classics or about other books on film, media and popular culture from BFI Publishing, please write to:

BFI Film Classics
BFI Publishing
21 Stephen Street
London W1T 1LN

BFI FILM CLASSICS

BFI Film Classics '... could scarcely be improved upon ... informative, intelligent, jargon-free companions.'
The Observer

Each book in the BFI Publishing Film Classics series honours a great film from the history of world cinema. With new titles published each year, the series is rapidly building into a collection representing some of the best writing on film. If you would like to receive further information about future Film Classics or about other books on film, media and popular culture from BFI Publishing, please fill in your name and address and return this card to the BFI.* (No stamp required if posted in the UK, Channel Islands, or Isle of Man.)

NAME

ADDRESS

POSTCODE

E-MAIL ADDRESS:

WHICH *BFI FILM CLASSIC* DID YOU BUY?

* In North America and Asia (except India),
please return your card to:
University of California Press, Web Department,
2120 Berkeley Way, Berkeley, CA 94720, USA

BFI Publishing
21 Stephen Street
FREEPOST 7
LONDON
W1E 4AN